What Is a Bird?

by Lola M. Schaefer

Chilean flamingo

Consulting Editor: Gail Saunders-Smith, Ph.D.

Consultant: Dwight Lawson, Ph.D.
General Curator, Zoo Atlanta

Pebble Books

an imprint of Capstone Press
Mankato, Minnesota

Pebble Books are published by Capstone Press,
151 Good Counsel Drive, P.O. Box 669, Mankato, Minnesota 56002.
www.capstonepress.com

2 3 4 5 6 06 05 04 03 02

Library of Congress Cataloging-in-Publication Data
Schaefer, Lola M., 1950–
    What is a bird?/by Lola M. Schaefer.
    p. cm.—(The Animal Kingdom)
    Includes bibliographical references (p. 23) and index.
    ISBN-13: 978-0-7368-0864-4 (hardcover)
    ISBN-10: 0-7368-0864-7 (hardcover)
    ISBN-13: 978-0-7368-9093-9 (softcover pbk.)
    ISBN-10: 0-7368-9093-9 (softcover pbk.)
    1. Birds—Juvenile literature. [1. Birds.] I. Title. II. Series.
QL676.2 .S37 2001
598—dc21   00-009669

Summary: Simple text and photographs present kinds of birds and
    their characteristics.

Note to Parents and Teachers

The Animal Kingdom series supports national science standards related to the diversity of life. This book describes and illustrates the characteristics of birds. The photographs support early readers in understanding the text. The repetition of words and phrases helps early readers learn new words. This book also introduces early readers to subject-specific vocabulary words, which are defined in the Words to Know section. Early readers may need assistance to read some words and to use the Table of Contents, Words to Know, Read More, Internet Sites, and Index/Word List sections of the book.

Table of Contents

Birds 5

Parts of a Bird 11

Flying 21

Words to Know 22

Read More 23

Internet Sites 23

Index/Word List 24

Birds are part of
the animal kingdom.
Birds have feathers.

wild turkey

Birds are warm-blooded.
Their body temperature
stays the same in
all surroundings.

Gentoo penguins

Female birds lay eggs in a nest. Chicks hatch from eggs.

pelican chick

Birds have a skeleton.
Their skeletons are made
of hollow bones.

scarlet macaw

Birds use lungs to breathe.

weaver finch

pied kingfisher

flightless pigeon

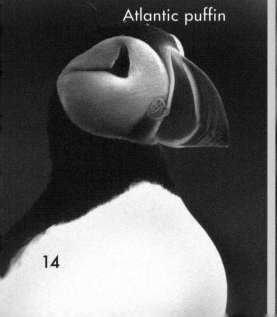
Atlantic puffin

bald eagle

14

Birds have a bill. Bills can be many shapes and sizes.

tail

Birds have a tail.

northern cardinal

wings

Birds have wings.

red-tailed hawk

Most birds can fly.

mallard

Words to Know

bill—the hard, pointed part of a bird's mouth; birds use their bills to eat, feed their young, and build nests.

chick—a young bird

feather—one of the light parts that cover a bird's body; some bird feathers are soft; others are fairly tough.

female—an animal that can give birth to young animals or lay eggs

hatch—to come out of an egg

hollow—to have an empty space inside; bird skeletons are made of lightweight, hollow bones.

lungs—a body part in the chest that animals use to breathe

skeleton—the framework of bones in the body of an animal or human

warm-blooded—having a body temperature that stays about the same, no matter what the outside temperature is

Read More

Burnie, David. *Birds and How They Live.* See & Explore Library. New York: DK Publishing, 1998.

Canizares, Susan, and Pamela Chanko. *Birds.* Science Emergent Readers. New York: Scholastic, 1998.

DeGezelle, Terri. *Birds A to Z.* Mankato, Minn.: Capstone Curriculum Publishing, 2000.

Internet Sites

FactHound offers a safe, fun way to find Internet sites related to this book. All of the sites on FactHound have been researched by our staff.

Here's how:

1. Visit *www.facthound.com*

2. Type in this special code **0736808647** for age-appropriate sites. Or enter a search word related to this book for a more general search.

3. Click on the **Fetch It** button.

FactHound will fetch the best sites for you!

Index/Word List

animal
  kingdom, 5
bill, 15
body, 7
bones, 11
breathe, 13
can, 15, 21
chicks, 9
eggs, 9
feathers, 5
female, 9

fly, 21
hatch, 9
have, 5, 11, 15
  17, 19
hollow, 11
lay, 9
lungs, 13
many, 15
most, 21
nest, 9
same, 7

shapes, 15
sizes, 15
skeleton, 11
stays, 7
surroundings, 7
tail, 17
temperature, 7
use, 13
warm-blooded, 7
wings, 19

Word Count: 71
Early-Intervention Level: 12

Editorial Credits

Mari C. Schuh, editor; Kia Bielke, cover designer and illustrator; Marilyn Moseley LaMantia, illustrator (page 12); Kimberly Danger, photo researcher

Photo Credits

Barbara P. Williams/Bruce Coleman Inc., cover (lower left)
Corel Corporation, 12, 14 (upper right)
Digital Stock, 14 (upper left)
Frederick D. Atwood, cover (lower right)
Index Stock Imagery, 10
Joe McDonald/McDonald Wildlife Photography, 4
Leonard Rue Enterprises, cover (upper right)
PhotoDisc, Inc., 1, 14 (lower left and lower right), 16, 18, 20
Visuals Unlimited/Maslowski, cover (upper left); Gerald & Buff Corsi, 6
Wendell Metzen/Bruce Coleman Inc., 8